# FIRST LESSONS *in*
# PIANO IMPROV

## A Basic Guide for
## Early Intermediate Pianists

*By Jeremy Siskind*

T0066155

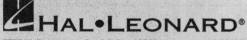

ISBN 978-1-4950-6260-5

# HAL•LEONARD®

7777 W. BLUEMOUND RD. P.O. BOX 13819 MILWAUKEE, WI 53213

In Australia Contact:
**Hal Leonard Australia Pty. Ltd.**
4 Lentara Court
Cheltenham, Victoria, 3192 Australia
Email: ausadmin@halleonard.com.au

Visit Hal Leonard Online at
**www.halleonard.com**

# PREFACE

## To the Student

We are often told that improvisation simply means making stuff up. While that is technically true, it is important to note that some improvisations are better than others. A good improvisation, like any good piece of music, should be rhythmic, cohesive, logical, and feel complete. This book demonstrates how to learn the rules of music through improvisation so that when you improvise, you are making up good stuff!

Whether you plan to be a composer, a jazz musician, or a classical pianist, improvisation is a great way to deeply learn the rules of music—to become a native speaker of musical language, rather than just a reader of notes. This book will guide you from very basic improvisational exercises through creating more complex melodies, generating varied accompaniments, and formulating longer phrases, up to improvising complete ABA forms.

## To the Teacher

Your involvement is critical to the success of this curriculum! You are the best person to introduce each idea, to practice call and response exercises with the student, to listen and assess a student's musical ideas, and to suggest creative alternatives that bring them outside their musical habits. Please make sure that each time a student practices an improvisational exercise, they are playing with excellent rhythm, a healthy amount of variety, and a specific goal in mind.

I often tell my students that learning to improvise is about learning strict rules...and then breaking them. This curriculum provides encouragement to the tentative improviser by giving ample guidance in the form of rules. As the book goes on, it gives the restless creator many opportunities to break from the original limitations. Because teaching improvisation is inevitably a balance between rules and structure (the *teaching* part) and unbound creativity (the *improvisation* part), you, as a teacher, have to strike a delicate balance. You might have to encourage the reticent student to stray from the examples or models; and, equally, you might have to rein in the creative student to adhere more closely to the given structure.

Regardless, I am excited for you to see the results of your students learning to improvise—not just in their creative output, but also in their understanding of musical form, their rhythm and phrasing, and their ability to listen critically to music of all genres.

Jeremy Siskind

# CONTENTS

## CHAPTER 1

# RHYTHM

# Imitation

As humans living on Planet Earth, **rhythm** constantly surrounds us—in footsteps, in heartbeats, in breathing, in keyboard clicks, and in a hundred other parts of our day. In fact, there are lots of ways that our bodies are percussion instruments. Have you ever slapped a knee or clapped your hands? That's percussion! Have you ever puffed out your cheeks and then popped them with your finger like a human balloon? That's percussion too!

Here is a rhythmic activity that uses your natural talents for percussion. First, pair up with a teacher, parent, or friend. Stand and march slowly together in place—*left foot, right foot, left foot, right foot,* etc. Let's define your teacher/partner as the "caller" and you as the "responder." The caller will have four footsteps—*left, right, left, right*—to perform rhythmic body percussion sounds; for example, slapping, tapping, popping, snapping, or stomping. As the responder, listen to the caller and copy the rhythm EXACTLY during the next four footsteps: *left, right, left, right.* Keep the beats steady, with no breaks between footsteps. We are practicing **imitation**.

If the rhythm was written out on a music staff, it might look like this:

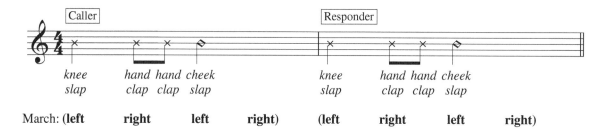

Or, like this:

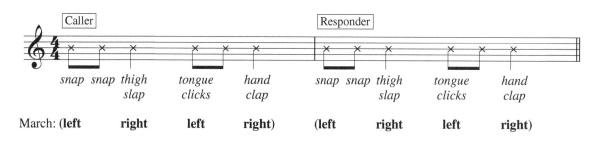

Repeat until copying becomes effortless. Then switch! You will be the caller and will come up with a rhythm that lasts for four stomps of the foot: *left, right, left, right.*

Next, practice repeating your partner's rhythms at the piano using one note. The caller will play a rhythm on the piano. Listen and then play the same rhythm back. Pick ANY note and remember that it is not necessary to play the same note as the caller. Keep marching with your feet while seated: *left, right, left, right*. Whatever rhythm the caller plays during these four footsteps, repeat exactly during the next four steps while marching *left, right, left, right*.

Your exchanges could look something like this:

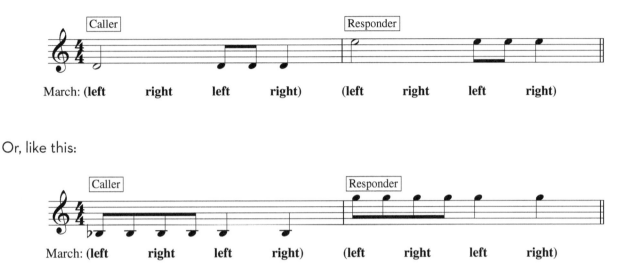

Or, like this:

Next, switch again. You will play the role of caller and will come up with an original four-beat rhythm on a single note at the piano. Again, limit yourself to four foot stomps: *left, right, left, right*.

## NEXT STEPS

1. Play the same game with two notes on one hand: one note with the thumb, the other with the pinky. Take turns being the caller. Copy not just the rhythm, but also pitches that are higher or lower. For example:

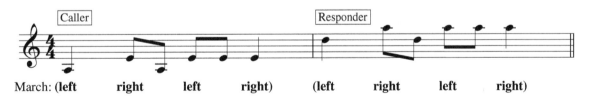

2. Play the same game with twice as many beats: eight footsteps for each player instead of four.

3. Incorporate dotted rhythms, rests, and triplets.

## CHAPTER 2

## MELODY

# Five-Finger Quarter Notes

**Melodies** are the part of the song that you can't get out of your head. They're the part that you hum in the bath or sing along with your friends when your favorite song comes on the radio. A great melody is something that you can sing and remember, a tune that's familiar but that maybe also surprises you a little bit.

Scales are the DNA of melody—each one contains millions of melodic possibilities. We will start by finding melodies using the first five notes of the C Major scale, also known as the C Major five-finger position. Place the right-hand thumb on Middle C and allow the other fingers to fall comfortably on each successive note:

Keep your fingers on these keys for an improvisation game: see how long you can play consistent quarter notes without merely going up and down the scale. The rules: no stopping and no repeating any note consecutively. What you play could look something like this:

As you play, remember:

1.  Aim for *clarity!* Don't just wiggle your fingers—put force and weight behind each note. Practice good technique with firm fingers.

2.  Skip around and play with as much variety as possible, *unlike* the following:

*Include more skips*

**3.** DON'T play the same note twice in a row:

*Avoid repetition*

**4.** Practice with a metronome and DON'T skip a quarter note:

*Don't skip a quarter note*

Start this game with the metronome at ♩=**100** and maintain constant quarter notes for a minute (or more). Continue playing at faster and faster speeds, aiming for a personal best!

## N E X T   S T E P S

**1.** Practice adding cross-unders below Middle C using your 3rd finger (B) and 2nd finger (A) in addition to C, D, E, F, and G.

**2.** Play the game using the entire C Major scale. Don't forget to check your fingering.

**3.** Play the game with the left hand. Put your pinky on the C below Middle C to access C, D, E, F, and G (thumb).

**4.** Play the game using consistent eighth notes or quarter-note triplets (instead of quarter notes).

## CHORDS

# Repeated Chord Accompaniment

Although melodies are often the most memorable parts of a musical piece, an interesting **accompaniment** is crucial to create a complete and noteworthy musical statement. Accompaniments help to set the mood of the piece, to determine which parts feel tense or relaxed, and to distinguish sections.

Play through the popular 4-measure chord progression below. Listen to the arc created by these chords: the harmony starts out relaxed, becomes increasingly tense as we get to measure 3, and then relaxes again at measure 4.

Just holding the chords would not be very interesting. Rhythm needs to be added to the progression. To begin, repeat each chord four times per measure, in quarter notes. This accompaniment sounds like a march:

Using the rhythmic improvisation skills learned in Chapter 1, you can create a chord accompaniment. Instead of tapping, slapping, and stomping, use your creativity at the piano and come up with different rhythms for this progression. For example:

Whatever rhythmic pattern you come up with, repeat it exactly in each measure until the end. For now, always end with a half note. Ending with a longer note will make the phrase sound complete. Here is another possible rhythm with a half-note ending:

Rests can also be used to create different rhythms. Play through the example below, which includes quarter-note rests:

**Now it's your turn!** Create rhythms using the same 4-measure chord progression above. Use eighth notes, quarter notes, half notes, dotted half notes, and rests. Maintain a total of four beats for each chord.

First, write out three possible rhythms below. Then practice improvising new rhythms without writing them down. To come up with ideas, return to the tapping, slapping, and clapping in Chapter 1 and apply those rhythms at the piano.

NEXT STEPS

1. Experiment with dotted rhythms and triplets to create unique accompaniments.

2. Create repeated accompaniments for the same chord progression using the right hand. Then play the accompaniments with both hands.

3. Learn and play the four-chord progression in all major keys.

# RHYTHM
# Rhythmic Call and Response

Improvising with rhythm can be like having a conversation. Often in conversations, someone asks a question and expects you to answer—this happens in music too! A musical conversation is known as **call and response**. To master the rhythmic art of call and response, we will practice tapping call and response phrases and then improvise them at the piano.

Here are a few ground rules:

1. The *question* phrase (call) and the *answer* phrase (response) should be the same length. The examples in this chapter will use two measures each of call and response.

2. The *question* phrase and the *answer* phrase should be related. Imagine if someone asked what your favorite color was and you answered, "Four!" That response would not fit their question. It is the same way with music—we have to pay attention to the question to come up with a fitting answer.

3. End all call and response answer phrases with a whole note or a half note (for now). A long note at the end indicates that the conversation is complete and functions as punctuation in a sentence.

Let's start with your partner as *caller* and you as *responder.* Tap out this example:

Can you hear how the part you tapped provides an answer to the first two measures?

There are many good answers to the same question. For example, if asked your favorite color, you might say red or blue or green or yellow. Tap these next two examples with a partner to hear more ways to answer the same musical question:

Here are two examples using a different call phrase. Tap these with your partner for practice. Because the call phrase uses eighth notes, it is natural for the answer phrase to also use eighth notes.

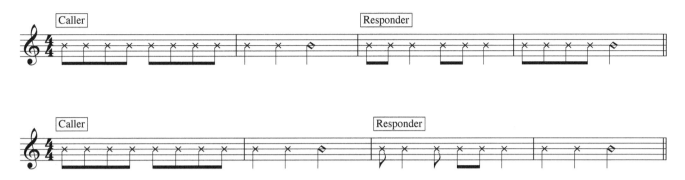

**Now it's your turn!** Your partner is going to tap the call rhythms provided below. Come up with a 2-measure response phrase. To prepare, write out possible response phrases on the staves below:

You are now ready to have a spontaneous conversation! Pair up and have your partner tap improvised 2-measure call phrases as you respond appropriately. Maintain a consistent pulse and listen carefully to be able to form suitable responses.

## NEXT STEPS

1. Practice improvising call and response phrases with your partner that are each four measures in length. End each phrase with a whole note or half note.

2. Practice call and response with yourself, tapping a question phrase with the right hand and an answer phrase with the left. Switch hands and repeat.

3. Improvise call and response rhythms using a single note at the piano.

## CHAPTER 5

## MELODY

# Melodic Call and Response

In this chapter, notes and pitches will be added to the **call and response** conversation. No chords will be added at this point, so it will be impossible to play a wrong note.

Start in C Major five-finger position. After your partner plays a call phrase, you can use any notes and any rhythm to improvise a response. In order to make the phrase sound complete, end each response on a whole or half note C.

Notice that the last two notes of the call phrase are repeated as the first two notes of the response phrase (although not in the same order). This repetition helps the two sound related. For example, if someone asked, "What's your favorite food?", you respond by starting your answer with the end of their question, "My favorite food is... pepperoni pizza."

Just like with rhythm, there are many melodic answers to the same melodic question. Play through the two examples below with your partner to hear other ways to respond. Determine how these phrases are related: Is it the notes? The rhythms? Both?

Play through the next two examples with your partner to hear some different examples of call and response. Can you determine how the phrases are related?

**Now it's your turn!** Your partner will play the three call phrases below and then you will come up with a response. Before improvising, write out two different response phrases for each call below:

You are now ready to have a spontaneous conversation. Have your partner play the call phrases on page 14 and improvise the responses. Then, have your partner improvise a two-measure call phrase and come up with a two-measure response in real time.

## N E X T   S T E P S

1. Practice call and response phrases on your own: play both the call phrase and the response phrase with your right hand to create a 4-measure improvisation.

2. Alternatively, practice call and response phrases on your own: play a call phrase in the right hand and the response in the left hand. Then switch hands!

3. Improvise call and response phrases all across the C Major scale. Use good fingering, and include cross-overs and cross-unders as needed.

## CHAPTER 6

## CHORDS
# Broken Chord Accompaniment

In Chapter 3, varied accompaniments were created by improvising new rhythms for blocked chords. Before we go on, remind yourself of our chord progression by playing through these chords again:

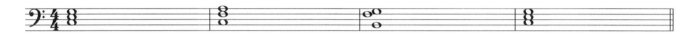

By playing the notes of the chord one at a time, a **broken chord** pattern is created in the left hand. Lots of music uses single-note broken chords—from Mozart sonatas to folk ballads to Adele hits. Depending on the tempo, broken chords can give the accompaniment a soothing flow or rhythmic momentum. Here's a way to play broken chords using only quarter notes:

This basic broken chord concept allows for the creation of many other rhythmic variations. A few examples follow below. All end on a half note to make the phrase feel more complete.

The notes of the chord do not have to be played in order. Experiment with jumping around from note to note. For example, instead of going directly from C to E, leap from C to G:

**Now it's your turn!** Create broken chord patterns different from the ones in the previous examples. Place longer notes on different beats or repeat some notes more than others. As usual, feel the beat and maintain a total of four beats for each chord. Write three ideas for broken chord patterns below. Then improvise new combinations without writing them down.

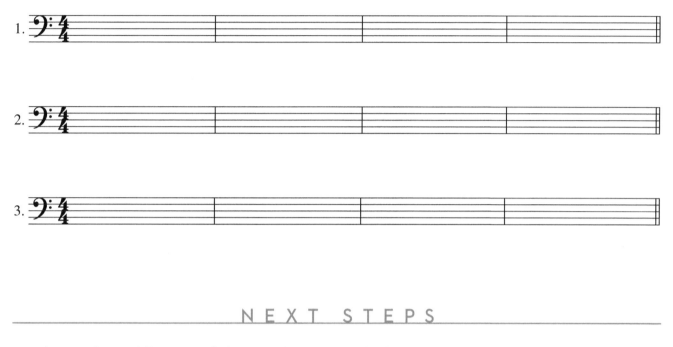

## N E X T   S T E P S

1.  Placing the middle note of the chord an octave higher can make broken chords sound more sophisticated and rich. Create new accompaniments utilizing this concept.

2.  Create broken chord patterns that place these chords in different inversions. Keep the inversions close to avoid leaping around from chord to chord.

3.  Experiment with broken chord patterns in different time signatures like 3/4, 6/8, and 5/4.

## RHYTHM

# Same Rhythm, Different Notes

The same rhythmic phrase can be used for different musical shapes. One way to create new melodies is to start with a rhythm.

Take the simple rhythm for "Twinkle, Twinkle, Little Star"—six quarter notes followed by a half note:

This rhythm could be the basis for hundreds of different melodies (including the rest of "Twinkle, Twinkle"). Here are four examples:

When creating a phrase based on rhythm, remember that you can:

1. Start on any note

2. Choose to go down, or stay the same

3. Use both steps and leaps (big and small)

**Now it's your turn!** Create phrases based on the "Twinkle, Twinkle" rhythm. Write out six new melodies that use the rhythm. Then improvise as many new phrases as you can using the same rhythm.

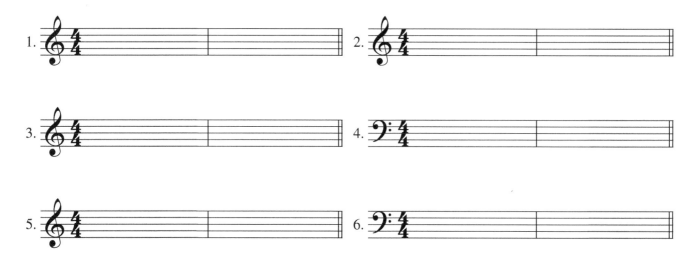

Different rhythmic patterns can be used as a starting point for improvisation. Below, you'll find several sample rhythms to use as starting points:

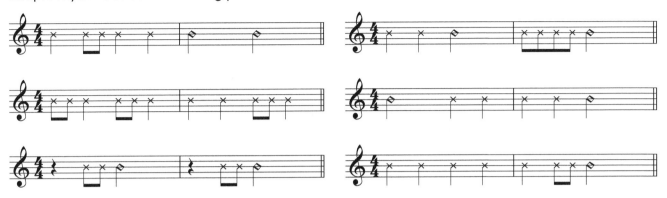

First, write out your own 2-measure rhythmic patterns on the staves below. Then, based on your rhythms, improvise new phrases while maintaining a consistent beat. Feel free to create your own rhythms or to borrow rhythms from a favorite song. Remember that it's a good idea to end each phrase with a half note or whole note to make it feel complete.

## NEXT STEPS

1. After creating a 2-measure rhythmic pattern, incorporate leaps of a fifth or larger into the melody.

2. Improvise new phrases based on rhythms that include dotted rhythms, syncopation, and/or triplets.

## MELODY
# Melodic Arpeggios

When notes in a chord are played separately, in ascending or descending order, this is called an **arpeggio**. It is similar to the broken chord accompaniment played in the left hand. Playing arpeggios in the right hand is one of the best ways to avoid *dissonances* (notes that create tension).

When holding a chord in the left hand, the right hand can create a melody by arpeggiating the notes that are in the chord. Practice improvising using arpeggios on the first chord of the progression (C Major, C-E-G).

Play the example below, then improvise a melody. Stick to C, E, and G and be creative with rhythm:

Even though there are only three notes, arpeggios can create stimulating melodies. Think of the opening notes to Beethoven's 5th Symphony, the Glenn Miller tune "In the Mood," or "Have Yourself a Merry Little Christmas."

Now, improvise using notes in the second chord (C-F-A, an F Major chord in inversion). Place the right hand in C Major 5-finger position, then stretch out fingers 2, 3, 4, and 5 to rest on E, F, G, and A.

Play the example below, and then improvise a melody:

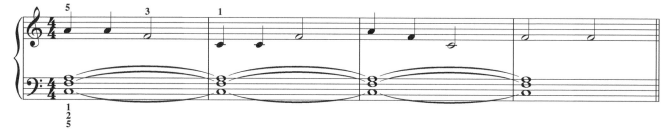

Lastly, practice arpeggiating the third chord (B-F-G, an inverted G dominant seventh chord). Reposition the right hand to the C Major 5-finger position. Now stretch the thumb down to the B below Middle C. Feel free to use the note D in addition to B, F, and G, because D is usually part of this chord and helps fill the big gap in the middle.

Play the example below, and then improvise a melody:

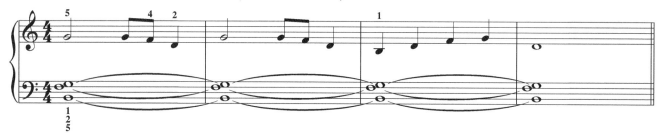

Notice that this chord feels tense. Its purpose is to lead back to the first C Major chord (C-E-G). If the unsettled sound drives you a little crazy, resolve both hands to a C Major chord after a few measures.

Once you feel comfortable improvising with arpeggios on each chord, practice improvising arpeggios over the progression in rhythm. For example:

**Now it's your turn!** On the staves provided, write out three 4-measure improvisations based on arpeggios. Remember that the right-hand arpeggio should match the notes of the left-hand chord. Then improvise phrases using right-hand arpeggios that match the left-hand chord progression.

**HINT:** It will help to think of the first two measures as a call phrase and the next two as a response.

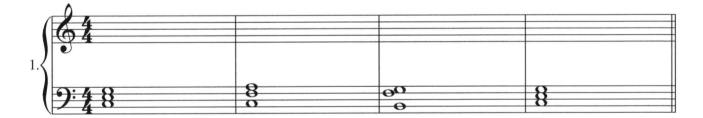

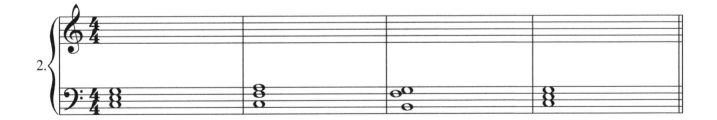

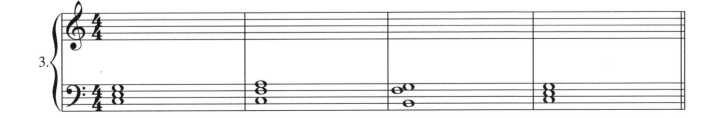

1. Improvise or write out melodies using arpeggios that span multiple octaves. Playing these will require well-thought-out fingering, especially when crossing over and under. For example:

2. Combine repeated chords in the left hand with arpeggios in the right hand. For example:

## CHAPTER 9

## CHORDS

# *Oom-pah* Accompaniment

**Oom-pah accompaniment** is a style used in genres like polka and ragtime. *Oom-pah* possesses an inherent dance feel because its bass notes fall on the strong beats, where a dancer would likely step.

Before practicing this style, play the basic chord progression once more:

Create the *oom-pah* left-hand pattern by separating the chord into two parts—the lowest (bass) note and the higher two notes. It is called an *oom-pah* pattern because the low bass note sounds like the syllable "oom," while the rest of the chord sounds like the syllable "pah."

Using the two parts of the separated chord, you can change the rhythm to create many more variations, including by changing the number of "ooms" and "pahs" to create a new accompaniment:

You can also use eighth notes instead of quarter notes to create a pattern with a greater sense of forward motion. It is still important to end the accompaniment pattern with a half note to achieve a sense of closure.

**Now it's your turn!** Create *oom-pah* patterns different from the ones in the previous examples. Mix the amount and placement of the "ooms" and "pahs" and get creative with the rhythm. Remember to feel the beat and to maintain a total of four beats for each chord. Write three ideas for *oom-pah* patterns below, and then improvise new combinations without writing them down.

## N E X T   S T E P S

**1.** Move the bass note ("oom") down an octave to create an accompaniment more like ragtime. This style of accompaniment is known as *stride piano*.

**2.** Place the bass note ("oom") up an octave so it is above the "pah" notes.

**3.** Hold the bass note ("oom") while playing the "pah" notes of each different pattern.

## CHAPTER 10

## RHYTHM

# Using Both Hands to Improvise
## (Together)

Ultimately, you want to be able to improvise with both hands together. To truly improvise with both hands requires high levels of focus and preparation because improvising with both hands requires thinking about two things at once! However, we are used to multi-tasking in our everyday lives. Most of us can walk and talk to friends at the same time, or ride a bike while thinking about our day; some students even claim that they are able to watch television while doing homework!

Coordinating the hands requires thoughtful consideration of how they fit together. From a rhythmic perspective, there are two ways to coordinate the hands:

1.  Play simultaneously

2.  Take turns

This chapter will focus on the hands playing simultaneously. Play through the arpeggiated melody below:

Next, practice playing hands together with all three accompaniment styles. First, with repeated chords:

Now, play with broken chords and *oom-pah*. These accompaniments might not sound amazing, but keep in mind that they are exercises to train coordination.

There is not one single correct way to play broken chords or *oom-pah* in this context. For example, the broken chord accompaniment could have looked like this:

To create the best-sounding accompaniment, choose different pitches for moments when both hands sound together. For example, don't put a C melody note together with a C in the accompaniment. Repeating the same note in the accompaniment will not create any harmony.

**Now it's your turn!** First, take the three melodies you wrote in Chapter 8 (page 21) and write accompaniments where both hands play simultaneously.

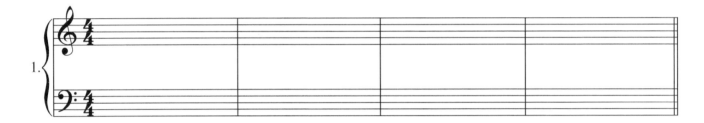

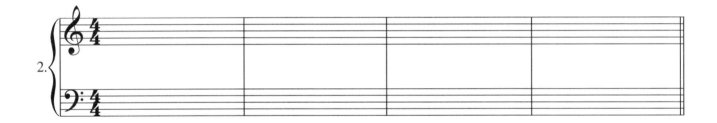

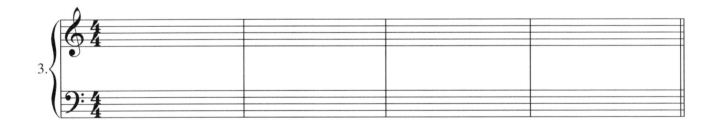

Then, improvise four-measure phrases with both hands, playing arpeggio melodies in the right hand with identical rhythms in the left hand.

1. Practice improvising with two measures per chord to create an 8-measure phrase.

2. Scramble the chords to create a different progression. For example:

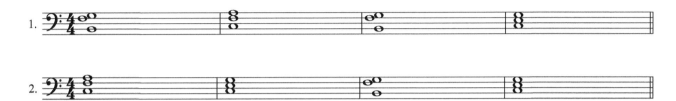

## CHAPTER 11

## MELODY
# Filling in the Scale with Passing Tones

Practicing right-hand arpeggios establishes a strong connection between chords and melody. As we add more notes to melodies, remember that the notes of the arpeggio are still the most important. They should *always* be:

1. The longest notes in the melody
2. The notes that fall on the downbeat (the first beat of the measure)

To add melodic variety, other notes of the scale are used *in between* the notes of the arpeggio. These types of notes are often called **passing tones**.

Here is the first 4-measure arpeggio melody from Chapter 8:

Play through the next example to hear the melody embellished with notes from the C Major scale:

Here is the second melody from Chapter 8. Again, it is based on an arpeggio:

Play through this next example of embellishment using notes from the scale:

Of course, you want to be able to improvise over a moving chord progression. The next example demonstrates a more complex melody over moving chords. Can you identify which notes are part of the arpeggio and which notes are filling in?

**Now it's your turn!** Take the three melodies you created in Chapter 8 (page 21) and embellish them by filling in the leaps with notes from the C Major scale. Then, improvise new melodies using the same concept. Remember that the melodies should have a precise rhythm that aligns with the chord progression.

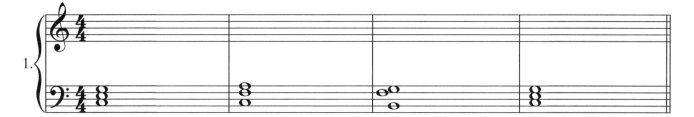

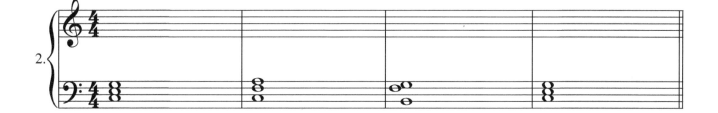

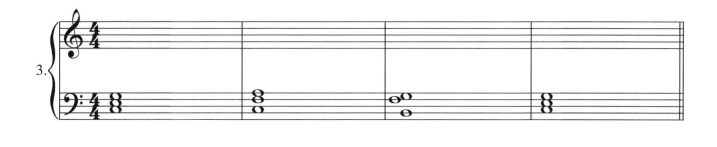

N E X T   S T E P S

1. Improvise 8-measure phrases (two measures per chord) using this melodic style.

2. Move one or both hands up an octave (or two) and experiment with different sounds and textures at the piano.

3. Fill in the melodies with chromatic notes (using ALL notes, not just the notes of the scale) for more unusual sounds.

## CHAPTER 12

## CHORDS

# Mixing Accompaniment Styles

The chord progression below should now be very familiar:

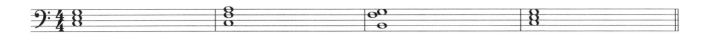

So far, we have covered three accompaniment styles: **repeated chords**, **single-note broken chords**, and **oom-pah**. Although we learned them individually, musicians often create variety by combining these accompaniments.

Changing the accompaniment style, particularly in the last bar of a phrase, can add to the finality of a phrase and help create a *cadence*, or musical ending. In the example below, *oom-pah* is used until the last measure, where it is replaced by a broken chord.

The opposite is also possible: try starting with a broken chord accompaniment and then changing to *oom-pah* for the last measure.

Accompaniment styles can also be mixed within a phrase. In the example below, repeated chords are used for measures 1, 2 and 4, and broken chords are used in measure 3.

**Now it's your turn!** Create mixed accompaniments by combining elements of repeated chords, single note broken chords, and *oom-pah* styles. Remember to feel the beat and maintain a rhythm of four beats per chord. Write out and play three accompaniments and then improvise new ones without writing them down.

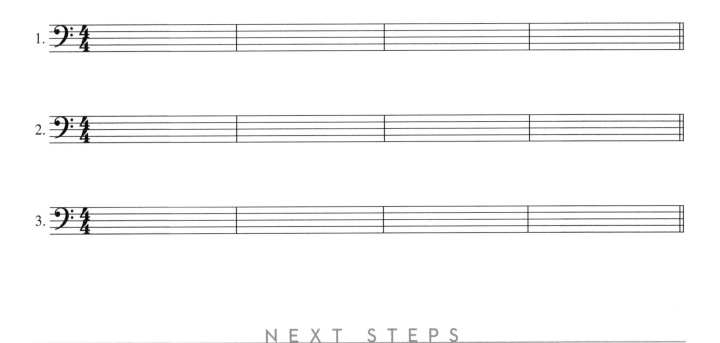

1.

2.

3.

## NEXT STEPS

1. Experiment with mixing accompaniments in the same measure.

2. Play the accompaniment in the right hand while improvising with the left.

3. Alter the F Major chord to an F Minor chord by changing the A-natural to an A-flat. This creates drama in the chord progression.

## CHAPTER 13

## RHYTHM

# Using Both Hands to Improvise
## (Staggered/Alternating)

In Chapter 10, you learned to play the left and right hands at the same time. In this chapter, you will practice doing the opposite—the hands will alternate (not play at the same time).

Look at the example below. The accompaniment was created by:

1. Placing a chord on beat 1 of every measure
2. Placing a chord on every eighth note where it does *not* line up rhythmically with a melody note (the chords will mostly fall on off-beats)
3. Ending with a chord on beat 3

This rhythm is more complicated than other rhythms learned so far, but it is an important exercise towards gaining rhythmic independence. Tap the rhythm on your lap before playing it on the piano:

Here is another example using a melody from Chapter 11. In this example, the chord does not change:

The next two examples demonstrate accompaniments created using single-note broken chords and *oom-pah*. Remember that there are many ways to create these accompaniments. You can decide for yourself what sort of shape to create.

**Now it's your turn!** On the staves below, write out the three melodies you composed in Chapter 8 (page 21) and create accompaniments in which the left hand plays in the rests or gaps left by the right hand. Then, improvise four-measure phrases with both hands, playing rhythmically staggered accompaniments in the left hand.

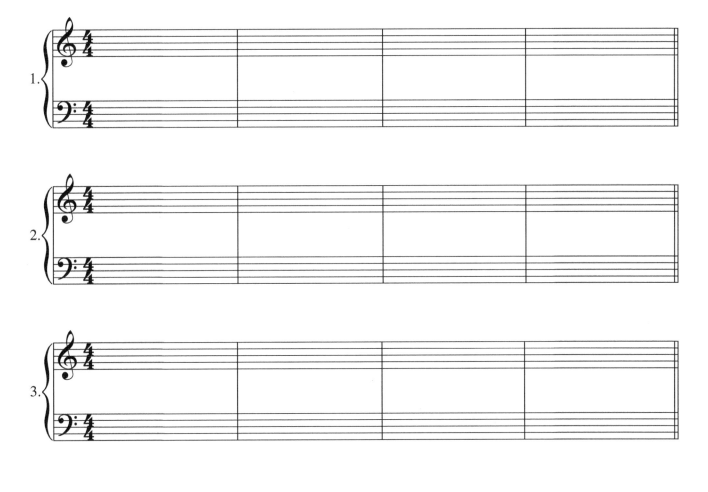

## NEXT STEPS

1. Experiment with alternating between the "hands together" approach of Chapter 10 and the "hands staggered" approach of this chapter. For example, play the first measure of each phrase with hands together, the second with hands staggered, etc.

2. Take a pre-existing left-hand accompaniment and compose, or improvise, a right-hand melody that complements the left-hand rhythm in a "staggered approach." In other words, form the improvisation backwards, starting with the accompaniment. Practice this concept with an accompaniment from Chapter 3, Chapter 6, or Chapter 9.

## CHAPTER 14

## MELODY

# Preparing for F Major and A Minor

So far, you have only been improvising in the key of C Major. A master improviser, however, can improvise in every key. A firm knowledge of the set of notes in every scale is critical as you continue to create new melodies and chords, so make sure to practice your scales regularly.

In this chapter, we will concentrate on **F Major** and **A Minor**, two keys closely related to C Major. Play through the F Major scale below with the correct fingering.

In F Major, the note to remember is the B-flat. To reinforce this new scale with the B-flat, return to the game from Chapter 2 but practice with the notes of the F Major scale. It may help to say "flat" every time you play a B-flat to remind yourself to play the correct black key. For example:

For more practice in a new key, revisit the exercise from Chapter 7: choose a one-measure rhythmic pattern and improvise new melodies using that rhythm choosing notes in the F Major scale. Two examples are shown below; the second is more active and meant for players looking for a challenge.

Now, turn to A Minor. There are a few different scales for A Minor, but our focus will be on the harmonic minor scale because it fits best with the chords we will be using.

Practice the rhythmic pattern exercises from page 34 in A Minor until you feel completely comfortable in the key. Notice that when in an A Minor 5-finger position, there is no need to worry about flats or sharps. Practice the rest of the scale and, just as you said "flat" for the F Major scale, it may help to say "sharp" when playing the accidental in A Minor.

**Now it's your turn!** Use the prompts below to write out repeated rhythms (on different notes) in these two keys. Practice improvising with these rhythms and then create your own.

## N E X T   S T E P S

1. Improvise in G Major and D Minor. Which accidentals are needed in order to make melodies in those keys?

2. Practice in these new keys with repeated 2- or 4-measure rhythms instead of the same rhythm in every measure.

3. Ask your teacher about (or do research on) natural minor, melodic minor, and harmonic minor. Compare and contrast the sounds of the different minor scales. What kind of character does each of the scales have?

## CHAPTER 15

## CHORDS

# Progressions in F Major and A Minor

You have now mastered the C Major chord progression below:

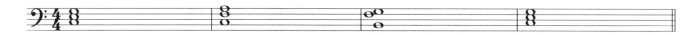

We can now begin mastering the same chord progression in **F Major**. In theory terms, the F chord is the *subdominant* of the C Major scale. Recall from Chapter 14 that the F Major scale has one flat in its key signature. Make sure to play all B-flats instead of B-naturals.

Play the F Major chord progression below:

**A Minor** is called the *relative minor* to C Major because both have the same key signature (no sharps or flats). However, when playing the chord progression in A Minor, add a G-sharp on the second to last chord, to create a *leading tone*; that is, a note that pulls upwards towards the A-natural. You practiced this in the A harmonic minor scale in the preceding chapter.

Play the A Minor chord progression below:

**Now it's your turn!** Experiment with these two progressions in the same way you did with the chords in C Major. Try different left-hand accompaniment styles and rhythms. Write out and play four accompaniment styles: two in F Major and two in A Minor. Then, improvise new variations in these keys without writing them down.

## NEXT STEPS

1.  Experiment with mixing chords from C Major, F Major, and A Minor. Which fit well together? Which don't?

2.  Form a complete 8-measure chord progression and include chords from all three keys. Use one chord per measure.

## CHAPTER 16

## FORM

# The 8-Measure Phrase

So far, we have been working exclusively with a 4-measure phrase. In order to achieve a more sophisticated sound, it is important to be able to connect two 4-measure phrases to form a complete **8-measure phrase**.

Here are a few suggestions to give an 8-measure phrase cohesion. For clarity, let's refer to the first 4-measure phrase as Phrase A and the second 4-measure phrase is Phrase B.

1. Use the same chord progression for Phrase A and Phrase B.

2. Start the melody of Phrase A and Phrase B in the same way.

3. End the melody of Phrase A on the 3rd or the 5th of the chord. Avoid the *root* (the note the chord is based on) here to keep the phrase from feeling like it's over.

4. Arrive at a melodic *climax* (the highest note of the melody) in the second measure of Phrase B.

5. End the melody of Phrase B on the root. This gives the phrase a sense of completion.

This may sound complicated, but it will get easier with practice. Play through the example below in C Major and listen for each suggestion above.

Here is another example in F Major. In measure 4, note that the 3rd and 5th of the chord are A and C. In measure 8, the root of the chord is F. Listen and watch for these markers.

**Now it's your turn!** Start by writing out three 8-measure improvisations: one each in C Major, in A Minor, and in F Major. Then, practice improvising 8-measure phrases in all three keys.

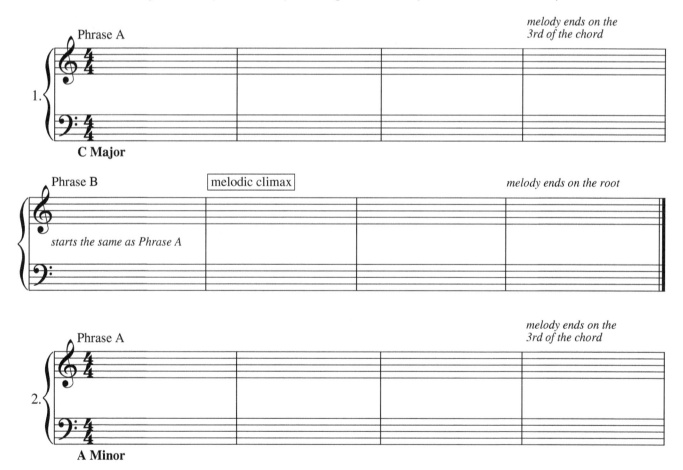

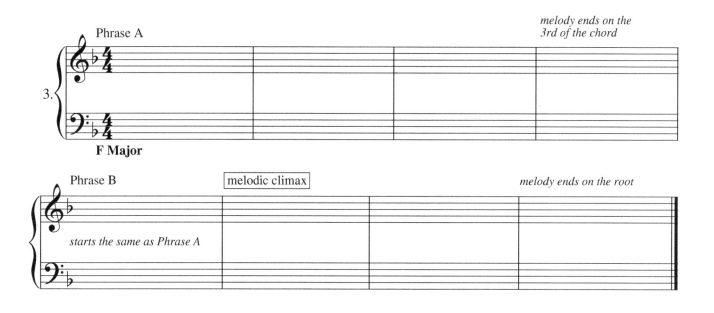

Phrase A

*melody ends on the
3rd of the chord*

3.

**F Major**

Phrase B

melodic climax

*melody ends on the root*

*starts the same as Phrase A*

## NEXT STEPS

1. Perform an 8-measure improvisation with the melody in the left hand and chords in the right.

2. Experiment with different right-hand articulations while playing an 8-measure improvisation, e.g. staccatos, two-note slurs, accents, etc.

## CHAPTER 17

## RHYTHM

# Waltz (3/4 Time Signature)

So far, we have been improvising in 4/4 time (four beats per measure). It is also common for music to be played in 3/4 time, with three beats in every measure.

One popular style in 3/4 time is the **waltz**, which is marked by a strong accent on beat one. Play through the common waltz accompaniment in *oom-pah* style below. The style features the root on beat one and the upper two notes of the chord on beats two and three.

Notice that in the example, the chords last for two measures so that they don't pass too quickly. With two measures per chord, each harmony lasts for six beats instead of three.

Broken chords work very well in 3/4 time: there are three notes in each triad and three beats in each measure. Play through the broken chord accompaniment below:

Just as with accompaniments in 4/4, you can make slight variations on waltz accompaniments. As you create variations of these accompaniments, make sure to include a strong accent on beat one to maintain the feeling of a waltz.

In the right hand, you can use all of the same devices you used in 4/4, except you have a little more time to do it—six beats for each chord instead of four. While filling in the melody with notes from the scale, remember that a note from the arpeggio (main chord) should land on the downbeat of each measure. Here is one possible improvisation:

**Now it's your turn!** Write out three 8-measure improvisations for both hands in 3/4: one in C Major, one in F Major, and one in A Minor. Then, improvise 8-measure phrases in 3/4 time.

1. C Major

2. A Minor

3. F Major

## N E X T   S T E P S

1.  Create accompaniments in six-beat patterns, where the repeated figuration is two measures long instead of one measure. For example:

2.  Create accompaniments in 3/4 time that require an extended hand position; for example, an *oom-pah* accompaniment with the bass an octave lower than the chords, or a broken chord pattern where the middle note is an octave higher than the rest.

3.  Alternate between 4/4 and 3/4 accompaniments to create a left-hand pattern in the unusual time signature of 7/4.

## CHAPTER 18

## MELODY

# Using Lower Neighbor Tones in the Melody

As a general rule, musicians use notes from the scale to create a melody. However, introducing notes from outside the scale can help to add character to a phrase. For example, think about the opening of Beethoven's "Für Elise" or the beginning of the Beatles' "When I'm Sixty-Four."

**Lower neighbor tones** are an effective way to introduce notes from outside of the scale. They are notes a half-step below a *chord tone* (a note from the triad/arpeggio). Lower neighbors return immediately to the chord tone.

Just as in Chapter 11, when you practiced filling in the notes of the scale, chord tones should still be placed on the downbeat and should be the longest notes in the melody.

Here is an example in the key of C Major with lower neighbor tones added to the melody line. The note a half-step below C is B, a member of the C Major scale. The note B functions simultaneously as a note in the C Major scale and as a lower neighbor tone. The D-sharp, F-sharp, and G-sharp are not in the C Major scale.

If a chord tone happens to be a black key, the lower neighbor will be the white key below that. The lower neighbors in the example below are related to the root chord in the key of F Major:

Here is a melody we have worked with before:

Lower neighbor tones can be used to embellish a melody. The addition of lower neighbors gives this melody a little more character:

To hear one more example, play through this melody from Chapter 17:

Now, play through the same melody with lower neighbor embellishments. Notice that it is generally the longer notes that are embellished, so that the shorter notes don't feel hurried.

**Now it's your turn!** First, write out three 8-measure improvisations using lower neighbor tones to embellish the melody. You can choose the key and time signature. Then, improvise in 8-measure phrases utilizing lower neighbors to embellish chord tones in the melody.

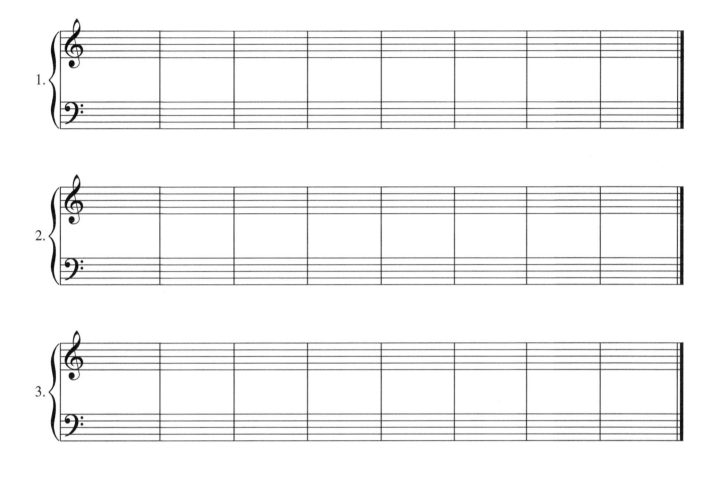

## NEXT STEPS

1. Can you improvise in the time signatures of 6/8 or 5/4? Can you improvise something that sounds like a march? A tango? Choose your own left-hand accompaniment to fit each style.

2. Experiment with using *upper neighbors*, embellishing chord tones with a note a half-step above. Which notes sound okay? Which sound funny?

3. Use lower neighbor tones to embellish the left-hand harmony. Experiment with using lower neighbors in accompaniment figures. For example:

## CHAPTER 19

## FORM

# Complete ABA Form

At this point, improvising in 8-measure phrases should feel reasonably comfortable. It is time to combine three 8-measure phrases to create a common 24-measure structure called **ABA form**.

An ABA form has two similar A sections. These sections share the same key, accompaniment style, and melodies. They are separated by a contrasting B section in a different key. The B section has a different accompaniment style and often possesses a contrasting *melodic character*. It might contain more long notes, short notes, leaps, lower neighbors, or rests than the melody in the A sections.

Here is an example of an ABA form in C Major. It modulates (changes key) to A Minor in the B section (measure 9). Carefully observe all the changes—accompaniment style, key, melodic character—that occur between the different sections.

In order to put these three sections together, a new chord was used to lead into each new key/section. Did you notice the chords on beat 4 in measures 8 and 16? These lead-in chords are technically called *V7* chords: they contain the *leading tone* to the new key. Here are three chords that lead into keys we have been practicing:

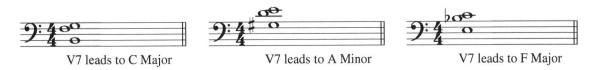

| V7 leads to C Major | V7 leads to A Minor | V7 leads to F Major |

The next example looks very different. Because it is in waltz form, it has twice as many measures (remember, each chord harmony lasts for two measures in 3/4 time). This example starts in the key of F Major for the A section and modulates to C Major for the B section (measure 17). Notice the different character of the A section—a busy melody using lots of neighbor tones—as contrasted to the B section—a slow, simple melody that exchanges a call and response with the left hand.

*(Continued on next page)*

In both examples, observe that a few different notes were added to the end of the last A section to make the ending sound more final. Inserting additional notes like this is a nice trick to let the audience know that the piece is coming to an end.

**Now it's your turn!** Use staff paper to write out 24-measure ABA improvisations (or 48 measures in 3/4 time), then improvise a few more on your own. I recommend writing out a basic plan before each improvisation that includes the key centers for each section, the V7 chords for each new key, the accompaniment patterns for each section, and any other elements you want to predetermine.

## N E X T   S T E P S

1. Experiment with different combinations of keys we haven't worked with. For example, G Major and D Minor, A-flat Major and D-flat Major, etc.

2. Explore other ways to create contrast between the A and B sections. For example, the texture: change octaves? Use a left-hand melody? Maybe an octave melody in the right hand?

3. Scramble the chords of the B section so that it starts on the V chord rather than the I chord. This helps to create a further contrast between the two sections.